I Have Cerebral Palsy

By MARY BETH SPRINGER

STAR BRIGHT BOOKS
CAMBRIDGE MASSACHUSETTS

Published by Star Bright Books in 2016.

The name Star Bright Books and the Star Bright Books logo are registered
trademarks of Star Bright Books, Inc.
Please visit: www.starbrightbooks.com.
For bulk orders, please email: orders@starbrightbooks.com,
or call customer service at: (617) 354-1300.

Printed on paper from sustainable forests.

Hardcover ISBN-13: 978-1-59572-750-3
Paperback ISBN-13: 978-1-59572-751-0
Star Bright Books / MA / 00105160
Printed in China / WKT / 9 8 7 6 5 4 3 2 1

Adaptive wheelchair and walker from Karman Healthcare.
Adaptive utensils as seen on Hubert.

Library of Congress Cataloging-in-Publication Data

Names: Springer, Mary Beth, author.
Title: I have cerebral palsy / by Mary Springer.
Description: Cambridge : Star Bright Books, 2016. | Audience: 4-10. |
  Audience: K to Grade 3.
Identifiers: LCCN 2016001957| ISBN 9781595727503 (hardcover : alk. paper) |
  ISBN 9781595727510 (pbk. : alk. paper)
Subjects: LCSH: Cerebral palsy--Juvenile literature.
Classification: LCC RC388 .S724 2016 | DDC 616.8/36--dc23
LC record available at http://lccn.loc.gov/2016001957

For Nannette, who has cerebral palsy and inspired me to write this book in recognition of her multiple accomplishments; for my daughter, Rebecca & grandchildren, who demonstrated how much fun it could be to think like a child; for friends & family who helped me to keep my dream alive; and especially for Sydney.

— M.B.S.

My name is Sydney and
I have cerebral palsy.

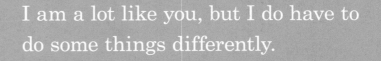

I am a lot like you, but I do have to do some things differently.

Cerebral palsy means that my brain has a hard time sending messages to the rest of my body. Cerebral palsy affects different people in different ways. For me, having cerebral palsy means that my arms and legs work differently than other people's.

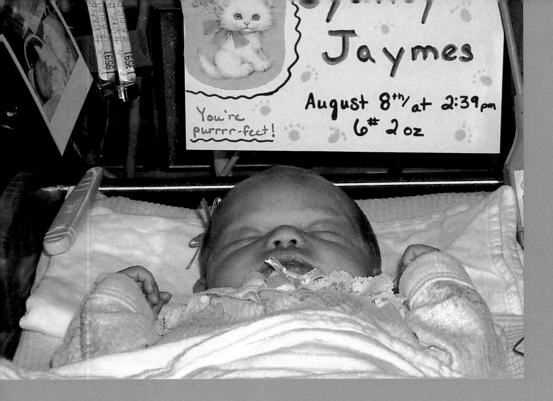

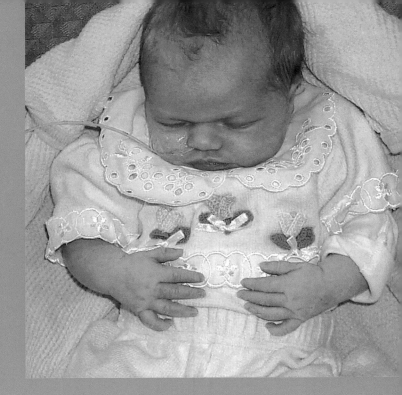

My brain was injured when I was born, but my parents—and the nurses at the hospital—thought I was purrr-fect, like all babies!

Like all babies, I slept a lot.

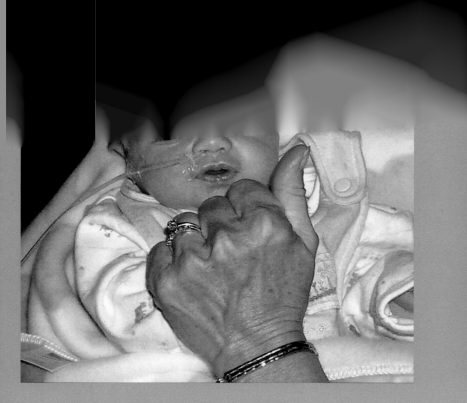

I loved people paying attention to me.

I did need a feeding tube to eat.
It didn't hurt and it helped me grow.

Having cerebral palsy is just part of my life.
As I grew up, I played with my toys and was
a messy eater—just like other babies.

When it snowed, my parents made a sled
out of a laundry basket. Sledding in the
snow was always fun.

Some of my other favorite things were swinging, playing with my dog, and reading books. Reading is still one of my favorite things to do.

Sitting up without help, especially
when I was small, is hard to do.

When I rode my new tricycle that
also rocked, I had to lean against the
handles.

Riding the merry-go-round was fun.
I wore a belt to keep from falling off,
but so did a lot of other riders.

I like helping out around the house. I felt important and special when I was helping my father build things with wood.

It's fun to go places with my family. I helped pick strawberries at a farm. We picked lots! I ate a lot too!

I may have trouble moving easily, but that has never stopped me from having fun. One of the things I enjoy best is water!

Even when I was a baby, I loved water!

In the summer, I always like to play in the swimming pool.

When my family and I go rafting on the river, I especially love going so fast that we all get sprayed by the water.

Learning to crawl and walk took me longer than other kids. When I try to move my arms and legs, I'm not always able to control my muscles the way I need to. So I learned to use a walker. A walker has wheels and when I walk, I lean on my walker and push forward.

I learned to climb the stairs using my arms and legs so that I wouldn't tip over. If I lost my balance and fell down the stairs, it would have hurt!

Riding a bike is fun. I had straps on the pedals to help my feet stay in place as I rode my bike.

Sometimes, especially at school or when shopping, it's easier to use a wheelchair. Not all people with cerebral palsy need to use a walker or a wheelchair. Some people may walk with a limp or need to use a cane or crutches to walk.

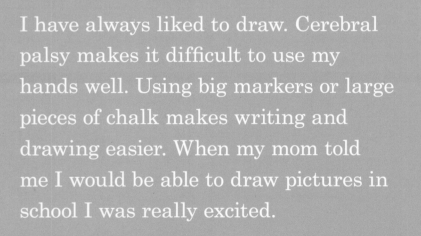

I have always liked to draw. Cerebral palsy makes it difficult to use my hands well. Using big markers or large pieces of chalk makes writing and drawing easier. When my mom told me I would be able to draw pictures in school I was really excited.

When I finally started school,
I felt grown up riding the bus.
The bus I ride has a special ramp
that works like an elevator so I can
get on and off the bus easily.

I love school! I can learn things like how to tie my shoes from my classmates. Everyone in my class wanted to know how my wheelchair works, and how I make it go in different directions so I showed them.

My classmates and I do all the usual things in school: we read books, do math, and have lunch together. It's fun when we have our reading group and take turns reading aloud.

Not all people with cerebral palsy have a hard time talking, but I do. I know what I want to say, but my brain may take a long time sending the words to my mouth.

I can understand what my friends are saying, but they may have to listen a little more patiently to understand what I am saying. We still enjoy talking together.

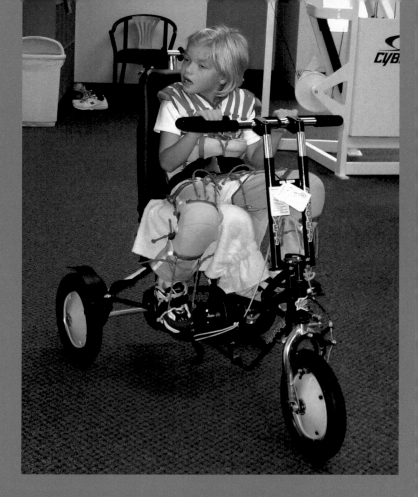

Cerebral palsy can make the affected muscles tight. I have physiotherapy to keep my muscles flexible.

The exercises I do help me have more control over my body.

When I can do what my physical therapists asks, I feel good about what I have accomplished. The harder I work at my exercises, the easier they are to do.

I love playing baseball. I play for the Miracle League, and my coach is also my "buddy." A "buddy" is a volunteer who helps each player with batting and running to the bases.

The specially designed baseball field is easy to move on in my walker. I like it when I hit the ball and get to go around the bases with my buddy at my side cheering me on.

I love the chance to dress up! I felt very special when I got to wear a crown of flowers and a white sash at a local fall festival. Even my sash says "Special!"

Sometimes, my family and friends help me decorate my walker to celebrate special occasions, like weddings.

See how I wrapped my walker in ribbons and flowers to match my dresses.

If you see my legs bouncing up and down, it means that my body is having a muscle spasm. It's kind of like when your arms or legs fall asleep and they "tingle."

I cannot stop my body from having muscle spasms. My arms might swing or my legs twitch. It might look strange, but don't be scared.

If you see me making strange faces, I might be having a muscle spasm in my face. When this happens, my eyes and mouth scrunch up like I have smelled or tasted something horrible.

Sometimes people who don't understand cerebral palsy laugh at me when they see me having a muscle spasm. This hurts my feelings.

I don't laugh at people who are different from me. Differences are what make people interesting!

Having cerebral palsy makes it hard to do some things, but I like to do the same things other kids do. I hope that if people read my story that they will be less shy when they meet another kid with cerebral palsy.

What Kinds of Adaptive Items Does Sydney Use?

Children with cerebral palsy, like Sydney, use everyday items that have been adapted to make it easier to do everything from walking to drawing.

Walkers: walkers come in all sizes and colors and make getting around easier.

Adaptive bikes: riding a bike is fun and no one should miss out on bike riding. For a child with cerebral palsy, there are bikes with high backs to support the neck and head. Pedals have straps to keep feet in place and a handle bar that is easy to grasp and maneuver.

When your hands don't hold objects well and your muscles don't move the way you want, there are lots of every day activities that become difficult to do. Activities like eating, getting dressed, and writing or drawing require the use of the small muscles in your fingers. This ability is called fine motor skills.

Think how tough it must be to eat if you can't control your fingers! Kids like Sydney can use specially designed bowls and cutlery.

See how the **bowl** has a curve? That's so you can scoop your food into a spoon or fork and it doesn't fall out of the bowl.

The cutlery–the spoon and fork–have handles that are large and ridged and easy to grasp.

Cups with handles make drinking easier.

Writing and Drawing

Devices that help someone like Sydney to write can be attached to pens or pencils for her fingers to grasp so she can write.

Large markers, crayons, and markers make drawing easier for kids with cerebral palsy. Large paintbrushes are also helpful.

Wheelchairs like Sydney's are designed to get her to where she needs to be and to be easy to operate. It is motorized, and Sydney drives it using controls on the arm of the chair. One of the tough things about being in a wheelchair is that you have to look up at people all the time. Sydney appreciates it when people sit down so they can talk without her having to crane her neck up.

To learn more about cerebral palsy, please visit these websites:

http://cerebralpalsy.org

http://www.cdc.gov/ncbddd/cp/index.html

http://kidshealth.org/parent/medical/brain/cerebral_palsy.html

To find items or resources for children with cerberal palsy, visit: www.karmanhealthcare.com or www.ucp.org

Photo courtesy of Rebecca Levine and The Miracle League of Massachusetts.

The Miracle League

Coach Eddie Bagwell, of the Rockdale Youth Baseball Association of Georgia, noticed that at each ballgame a boy with spina bifida, a condition affecting the spine, cheered from the bleachers. Believing that every child should have the chance to play baseball, Coach Bagwell invited him to join the team.

In 1999, local children with disabilities were invited to join a baseball league of their own. While all the kids had a great time playing, it became apparent that it would be easier for the team members to play on a handicap-accessible field. A local Rotary Club raised funds to build the first custom-designed playing field for the Miracle League. These fields are completely flat so that kids in wheelchairs move easily, and kids with visual impairments can play without fear of tripping.

Miracle League volunteers are known as "buddies." Kids and adults can volunteer to be a buddy. Buddies help kids play and they cheer on all players. Being a buddy is a great way to enjoy baseball and help kids enjoy America's favorite pastime!

To lean more about The Miracle League, please visit the following websites:

http://www.miracleleagueofma.com

http://www.themiracleleague.net